Intro to Starting Your Business
By
Joseph A Nappi

INTRODUCTION

My name is Joseph; I am a Certified Business Coach living in Tampa Bay, Florida. I have started a couple of companies over the last decade from construction to trash removal and even my current coaching business. I am not a certified public accountant nor am I an attorney, so please don't take this book as legal advice. This book is meant for the purpose of ideas based on my education and business experience. I will be discussing topics from choosing your business name to structuring your business. I will also touch on marketing ideas and setting up your bookkeeping and Human Resources departments. Please enjoy this book!

Thank you and good luck on your venture!

Joseph A Nappi

Chapter 1

What is your passion? What do you enjoy doing? You might be a back yard gardener that is thinking of becoming a professional florist. Somewhere in the world there is a person that loves to work on their house and wants to become a professional handyman. Whatever your passion might be, you want to turn this wonderful passion into a business but you have no business experience and you don't know where to start.

Now that you have chosen a passion, you need to come up with a business name. If you don't have a name already chosen, let's think about how we can come up with one. I recommend a name that describes your company. For example, my first company that I started was called "Wild side Entertainment". I have chosen to add entertainment to the name to sort of give an idea of what my company was about. To be specific, this company was a music company that published songs and I could have been more specific by naming my company "Wild Side Music" but I was hooked on the name and didn't want to change it.

Another company that I started was "Luxurious Cabinets LLC" and this company was based in Findlay Ohio. I was very specific when I named this business because I used cabinets in the name. My business card had kitchen cabinets on it and it couldn't have been more obvious that this was a kitchen cabinet business. The other business that I created in Findlay, Ohio was "NAPCO WASTE CONTROL." Now I wasn't very specific with this name because this could have meant a few different things. I knew that once I marketed my business, people would know that this was a trash removal business and I chose the name because I liked it.

So if you like the business name, go with it. It can be specific to your product or service or it can have no meaning to your product or service. Let me bring up my business "Luxurious Cabinets" as an example that this is specific. On the other hand, naming your company something like "Orange Pro" can mean a lot of things, so get ready to do a lot of marketing and a lot of explain to why you chose a nonspecific name. But honestly, be a rebel and be creative. It is your business and this business might become your life's work.

Go name your business and use the lines below to write your ideas down. Try to come up with a few different ideas for business names.

_____

_____

_____

_____

_____

_____

_____

Now that you have your business name picked out, go on your State's "Secretary of State" website and search the name for availability. I recommend you either use a legal service to structure your company or just do it yourself, but before you decide who will incorporate your business, pick out a type of structure for your company.

Doing Business As a sole proprietor or using a fictitious name is the cheapest route but could be the dangerous route too. Basically, your company and your personal assets are all the same. This means that a customer can take you to court and sue you for everything between your business and you're personally owned assets like your automobile or even your home. I don't know why this is even an option any more. Plus when the owner suffers a death, the business dies with the owner.

The S-corporation and the C-corporation are popular picks. The S corporation protects the owners from losing personal assets. The S-corporation is a totally separate entity and will live on after the death of the owners. The S-corporation allows up to 25 shareholders in the State of Florida and is popular for single owners who want to protect their personal assets. I have personally chosen the S-corporation and I recommend looking into this type of business structure with an attorney or Certified Public Accountant.

Just like the S-corporation, the C-corporation is very similar but allows for unlimited shareholders or owners. This structure is a good choice for when your business is expanding and you are looking for investors. The last type of business structure I want to touch on is the Limited Liability Company. The owners are called members and there can be unlimited members or this can be a single-member owned LLC. Please feel free to do some more extensive research on your State Secretary's website and even contact a lawyer for a consultation on which type of business structure may be best for your business goals.

Please take some notes if you need too!

_____
_____
_____
_____
_____
_____
_____
_____
_____
_____
_____
_____
_____
_____
_____

Before I end Chapter 1, I will touch on the business plan. The business should include all of your information and goals. The business plan answers questions like how much your products and services will cost. If you intend not to try and scope out investors, then don't worry about a business plan. I typically do not write a business because I am not looking for investors and bank loans. It is entirely up to you!

CHAPTER 2

I am assuming that it is just yourself working but you need to hire help right away, lets discuss Human Resources. As a brand new entrepreneur, you will be the manager of many departments. You will be the sales manager, the accounting manager, and yes you will be the Human resources manager or better known as the HR manager. You will need to figure out how many employees will be needed and how much money you will pay your employees. You will have to do some internet research on fair wages for your specific industry. I know that in my kitchen cabinet industry, laminators are making 15 dollars an hours, saw cutters are making up to 25 dollars an hour and sales representatives are making 10-20 percent on each sale. Please research fair wages and be competitive because employees will come and go, especially for higher salary.

On top of salary, let's talk benefits. Are you going to offer health insurance to your employees? What about sick time and paid time off? Will there be any perks to working for your company?

You need to stand out when recruiting good employees. On the other hand, you will have a new business to run and probably are not going to be making a profit for a couple of years, so take it easy on the HR topic. Talk to your CPA or Attorney about employment laws because you don't want to make a mistake and cost your business its existence. Chapter 2 is not meant to scare you but inform you that you need to consult about these serious topics like employee laws.

As a business owner paying employees on the books, you will need to withhold payroll taxes. This may include social security tax, Medicare tax, unemployment premiums, and worker's compensation insurance. Please talk to your CPA and if you are going to perform services like bookkeeping and payroll by yourself, use software that does all the calculations for you. For example there is QuickBooks, and this service will help with bookkeeping and payroll for a monthly fee.

Recruiting is going to be vital while you find your first employees. Some entrepreneurs will find employees through friends and family, others will have to recruit through some sort of means like the internet. Honestly, your company is small and brand new. I would post an advertisement in the local paper or even maybe post a Facebook post on your Facebook business page if you have one.

You will also have to consider the experience level of your future employee. If you are a florist, are you looking for another experienced florist? Are you looking for a cashier for your floral shop?

Ask yourself these questions and use the space below to write your answers.

Are you looking for a fulltime employee or a part-time employee?

_____

_____

Will your employee be a professional like a carpenter or a florist? Or will your employee be more entry level like a cashier or a sales floor representative?

_____

_____

_____

What kind of benefits can you offer your employee right away to make your company look more appealing than your competitor's company? Hint: Healthcare, sick time, Paid time off..._____

_____

_____

_____

How will you recruit this employee? Do some research on local newspapers and write down 3 newspapers that you will call and get advertisement rates for.

- _____
- _____
- _____

Please use the following space below to make any notes or questions on Human resources.

_____
_____
_____
_____
_____
_____
_____
_____

_____
_____
_____
_____

CHAPTER 3

In this chapter, I want to touch on taxes, bookkeeping, and paperwork. My advice as I stated earlier in this report was to use software for your bookkeeping needs. Software is made to make no mistakes, you enter the information and it gets stored. When you need a report, just hit print and it prints out the report all figured out. If you hire a certified public accountant, this professional might use software as well, so save yourself money and purchase the software.

Save all of your receipts!!!

Save all of you receipts because you will need them if you don't want to pay taxes on all of your revenue. Save your gas receipts, material receipts, vehicle loan payment receipts, etc… Please track your mileage as well because each mile is tax deductible when you use a vehicle for business. For example, your total sales revenue for the year is 75,000 dollars. If you have no receipts to show the IRS then you will pay a percentage of 15 percent in taxes and that adds up to 11,250 dollars. Now if you have a total of

25,000 dollars in expenses from mileage and receipts you will only end up paying taxes on 50,000 dollars and your new tax bill would come out to 7,500 dollars.

That's a total of $3,750 you didn't have to pay the Government because you......SAVED YOUR RECEIPTS.

On top of saving expense receipts, you should be saving paperwork from any government agency like the IRS and any licensing boards that you may be communicating with if you are a licensed professional. You should have an organized folder with your licenses, insurances, and other paperwork like asset titles. Be prepared to show proof of insurance or proof that you are a licensed contractor. So save and organize your paperwork.

Please take some time and answer the questions below to better prepare you in owning your own business.

What kind of bookkeeping software will you purchase? What is the monthly quote for this service?

_____

_____

_____

What kind of expenses will you have during the business year? Think about vehicle maintenance, gasoline, materials, shipping costs, and many more expenses like office rent and internet service. List some expense your business will endure.

- _____
- _____
- _____
- _____
- _____
- _____

Make any other notes here that you need to make on expenses, taxes, and bookkeeping

_____

_____

_____

_____

_____

_____

_____

_____

_____

_____

_____

_____

_____

_____

_____

CHAPTER 4

This is one of my favorite chapters because it is covering marketing. Marketing is about making your business known by creating a brand for your business. There are many types of ways to market your business. You can market your business through Social Media, which is the most popular way in today's time. When it comes to social media marketing, we can agree that this may be the best way to get your business known to the public. You can use Facebook, twitter and many other social media sites to market your business.

Facebook is easy because you can make a business page about your business and then start an ad campaign through Facebook ads for as low as 5 bucks. People will see your advertisements in their news feed and if it is appealing enough they will click on your ad and like your page. This sounds like an affordable way to market your business in my opinion.

What is some social media websites you might market your business through?

- _____
- _____
- _____
- _____

Websites are great for promoting your business. They act like the headquarters of information for your business. Your website should consist of different pages. For example, you should have a home page which is your cover page and an about page where your business biography will be available for your customers to read. You should also consider having a products page or a service page where you list your services for your customers to see.

Please take some time here and check out some different websites from other companies in the same industry as your business.

Then take some time to write down the titles of the pages that will be on your website

- _____
  _____

- _____
  _____

- _____
  _____

- _____
  _____

- _____
  _____

- _____
  _____

- _____
  _____

- _____
  _____

- _____
  _____

- _____
  _____

Some other things to think about are logos, trademarks, and slogans. These can be creative artistic designs that will get your business noticed by the public. Graphic designers can create a logo for your business for a fee. You can also take some time to think about a logo or a slogan. Think about what the mission statement and the vision statement is for your business then take it from there and be creative about it.

Use the space below to make notes on any ideas you might have on logos and slogans

_____

_____

_____

_____

_____

_____

_____

_____

_____

_____

_____

_____

      I also wanted to include a list of other marketing material that you can use to help market your business:

- Business cards
- Post cards
- Flyers
- Presentation folders
- Car wrapping and door magnets

CHAPTER 5

Anyone entering into their own business should always have business goals. You have to ask yourself, where do you want to be in 5 years and what necessary steps should you take to get there? For example, you want everyone in town to know that your new business is open for their convenience. One of your goals should be to market your business strongly. You need to write a plan on how you are going to market your business and get the word out. So break down the large goals into smaller goals that will gradually take you to achieve your large goals. So you want to make your business known. Instead of just advertising in a small 2 inch by 2 inch advertisement in the paper, you should think about investing in purchasing a full page color advertisement. Taking steps like using full page advertising will get noticed more by the community and your business will be known by a larger crowd because the full page is more noticeable than a smaller advertisement.

It is also important to figure out your strengths and weaknesses in your business. To give a good example, when I became a licensed contractor, I wasn't experienced in every single step of the process. I knew that I couldn't cut on the table saw; I recognized this as a weakness. As an entrepreneur starting a kitchen cabinet contracting business, I figured that I would need to fill in all of my weaknesses. Of course, sometimes when starting a business you will not be able to afford to hire employees. In order for my business to start off strong, I hired an experienced table saw cutter. This allowed my business to run smoothly without problems because I couldn't cut on the table saw.

I gave up some of the profits in the beginning. I was able to hire a table saw cutter for about 18 dollars an hour. This move killed my chance of making a decent profit in the beginning but allowed me to make money once my sales took off. Sometime you have to compromise a little bit to get the business running. Now if you are starting a florist business, you probably are a passionate florist and you can start your business off by yourself. I was able to design kitchens, sell kitchens, build kitchens, and install kitchens. I just couldn't make the cut on the table saw.

Another area I wanted to touch on is bringing in a business partner. This can be good and it can be bad. I was very unfortunate to have a couple of bad business partners. You have to be on the same page as your business partner. I wanted to take some of the profits from one of my businesses and invest in marketing but my partner needed the money and literally wanted to split everything down the middle after the expenses were paid. This forced me to take my half of the business profits and invest in marketing and at the end, more business came our way but ended up in failure because every profit had to be cut down the middle and there just wasn't any way I can afford to market the business on my profits alone and pay my bills. Long story short, the 2008 recession came and I quickly dissolved that partnership and won't ever look back. It is best to make sure both you and your partner probably have an actual written plan on everything from expenses to marketing.

Notes

_____
_____
_____
_____
_____
_____

OUTRO

I hope this business guide will help you turn your passion into a business. Please review this guide as needed and good luck to you and your future business. Another quick tip from me; no one will ever know it all. You will probably need to read a few more books on business and get yourself a mentor. Please add my email to your contacts and reach out if you need any business coaching or consulting. I will be more than happy to work with you.

Joseph.nappi@gmail.com

Best of luck!

Joseph A Nappi